YES I HAVE WEDDING DREAMS

Copyright © 2021 by Yes I Have Anxiety, Inc.

All rights reserved.

Thank you for purchasing an authorized edition of this book and for complying with copyright laws by not reproducing, scanning, or distributing any part of it in any form without permission.

Consumer Use Disclaimer: The "Yes I Have" book series was created in light-hearted, relatable fun to create distractions from things individuals may be dealing with. All "Yes I Have" books are not intended to diagnose medical conditions nor provide a cure for any medical conditions. This book is not meant to be a replacement for real medical intervention if needed.

ISBN: 978-1-7364840-7-4

First Edition: December 2021

Yes I Have Anxiety, Inc.
Grove, Ok 74345

This book is dedicated to the original Founder of Yes I Have Books – surprise Nicole! She is getting married in March of 2022 to her best friend Evan. She is so deserving of the best life, security, and peace of mind. We are so incredibly proud of you! You are going to be the most beautiful bride! We can't wait to share this very special day with you!

We love you so much,

Mom and Natilee

> Don't be a Bridezilla.
>
> Come up with 10 Things a Bridezilla Would Do.

1.

2.

3.

4.

5.

6.

7.

8.

9.

10.

Paint Your Color Swatches Here, Pick Three, and Then Use Those Three Colors on the Next Page!

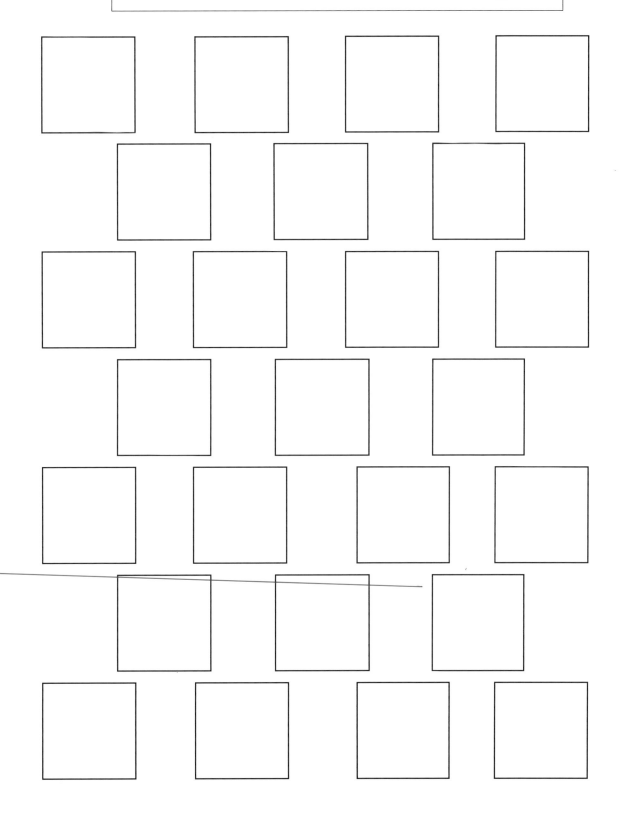

Use this Page as Your Wedding Inspiration Board.

(Glue Pics, Write Ideas, Jot Notes, Etc.)

Create a Wedding Budget.

You have $_____ to spend.

Total Expenses	Estimated	Actual

Apparel	Estimated	Actual
Rings		
Dress/Tuxedo		
Total		

Decorations		
Ceremony Venue		
Reception Venue		
Total		

Gifts		
Attendants		
Other		
Total		

Flowers		
Bouquets		
Boutonnieres/Corsages		
Ceremony		
Reception		
Other		
Total		

Music		
Music for Ceremony		
Music for Reception		
Other		
Total		

Photography		
Formal Photos		
Videography		
Other		
Total		

Reception (excluding music and decorations)	Estimated	Actual
Room/hall fees		
Tables and chairs		
Food & Drinks		
Linens		
Cake		
Favors		
Staff and gratuities		
Other		
Total		

Stationery / Printing		
Invitations		
Thank-you cards		
Guest book		
Programs		
Total		

Transportation		
Limos		
Parking		
Other		
Total		

Other		
Officiant		
Ceremony site fee		
Wedding Coordinator		
Rehearsal Dinner		
Engagement Party		
Showers		
Salon appointments		
Bachelor/ette parties		
Hotel rooms		
Total		

Wedding Guest List
(Who Makes the Top 25?)

Name	Street, City, State, Zip	Invited to Ceremony	Reception	R.S.V.P. Number Attending
1.				
2.				
3.				
4.				
5.				
6.				
7.				
8.				
9.				
10.				
11.				
12.				
13.				
14.				
15.				
16.				
17.				
18.				
19.				
20.				
21.				
22.				
23.				
24.				
25.				

Think Wedding and Complete the Crossword.

Across
2. A party usually held after the marriage ceremony.
5. Close friend or relative of the groom.
8. A woman whose behavior in planning her wedding is regarded as obsessive or demanding.
9. This is the man getting married.
10. Something old, something new, something _____, and something blue.
12. Typically walks down the aisle before the bride scattering flower petals.
13. Say Yes to The Dress.

Down
1. These are traditional promises exchanged between the couple during the wedding ceremony.
3. You cut this at the wedding.
4. This is the person who assists the bride in the lead up to the wedding.
6. A girl's bestfriend.
7. What does a man/woman propose with?
11. This is the woman who is getting married.

Make a Centerpiece for the Table.

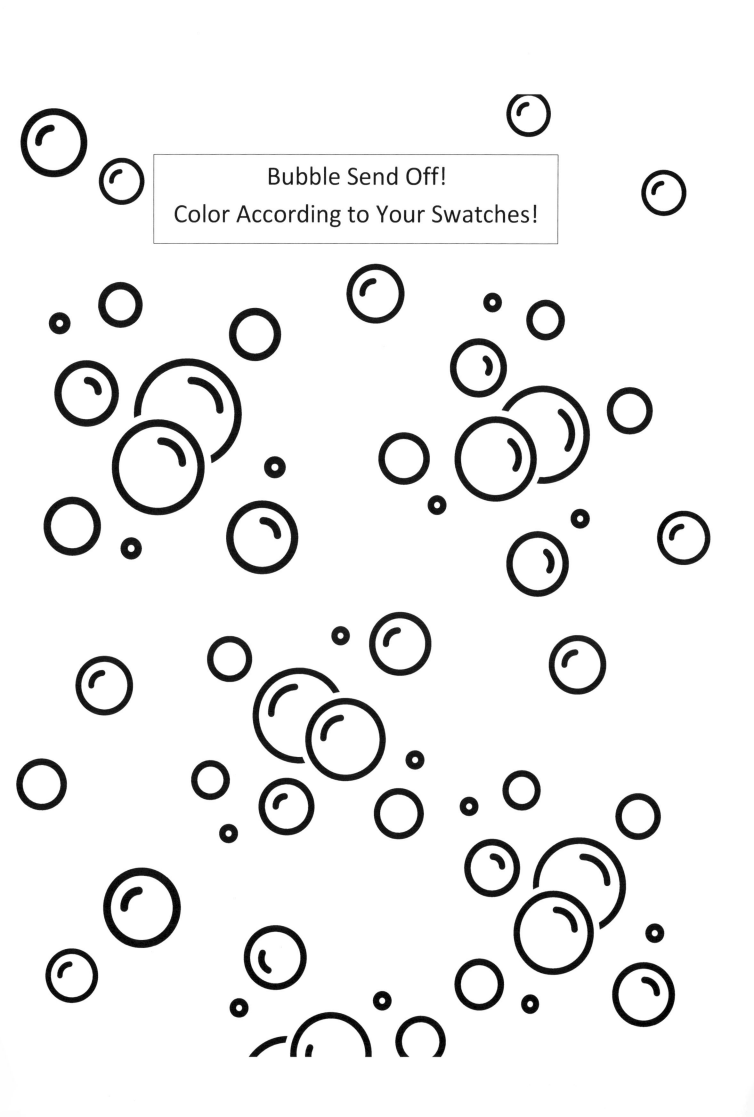

What Does Your Dream Cake Look Like?

#BrideTribe

Who are Your Bridesmaids? What are They Wearing? Glue Some Inspiration Below Their Names.

1. _____
2. _____
3. _____

4. _____
5. _____
6. _____

Here Comes the Bride!
Glue Your Flower Petals
to This Page!

Grab Some Toilet Paper and Glitter to Make the Veil Sketch Come to Life!

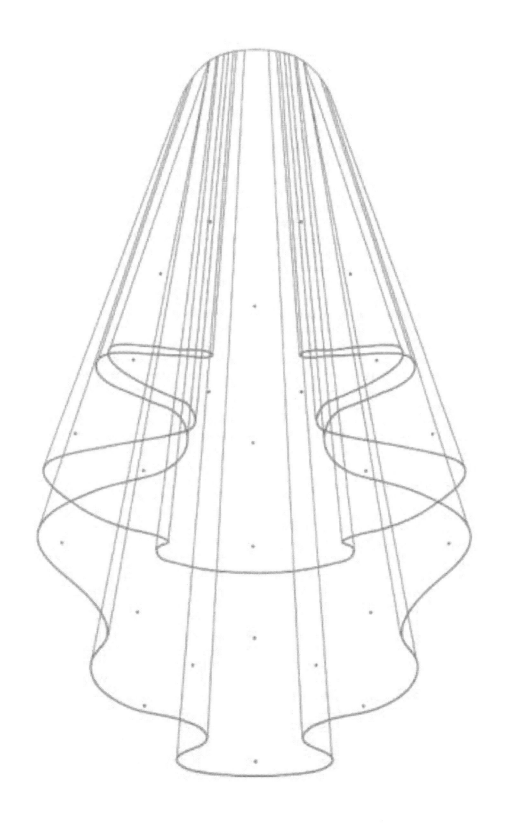

Create a Dramatic Wedding Dress Using Feathers, Q-Tips, Etc.

What is the Vision? Fill Out the Questionnaire Below!

Select Three Words from the Following List That Best Describes Your Wedding Day Vision:

Elegant	Grand	Glamorous	Rustic	Conservative
Simple	Traditional	Contemporary	Country	Modern
Party	Romantic	Funky	Magical	
Celebration	Sophisticated	Vintage	Festive	

Other Words Not Listed That Describes Your Wedding Day Vision: _____

Wedding Colors That You Vision for Your Wedding Day:

_____   _____   _____
_____   _____   _____

Wedding Cake Style: _____   **Season/Date:** _____

Favorite Winter Flowers (Choose Two):

| Amaryllis | Carnations | Orchids | Daisies |
| Baby's Breath | Cattleya | Chrysanthemum | Roses |

Favorite Spring Flowers (Choose Two):

Amaryllis	Cattleya	Forget-me-knot	Lily	Ranunculus
Anemones	Daffodils	Gardenias	Lily of the Valley	Roses
Baby's Breath	Day Lily	Iris	Larkspur	Sweet pea
Calla Lily	Delphinium	Jonquil	Orchids	Tulip
Carnations	Freesia	Lilac	Peony	Violets

Favorite Summer Flowers (Choose Two):

Aster	Calla Lily	Daisies	Iris	Stephanotis
Baby's Breath	Canterbury	Day Lily	Larkspur	Straw Flowers
Bachelor	Carnations	Delphinium	Lily	Zephyr Lily
Bells	Cattleya	Geranium	Orchids	
Buttons	Chrysanthemum	Hydrangea	Roses	

Favorite Fall Flowers (Choose Two):

Aster	Calla Lily	Chrysanthemum	Delphinium	Zephyr Lily
Anemones	Carnations	Daisies	Orchids	Zinnia
Baby's Breath	Cattleya	Day Lily	Roses	

Ceremony Location (Circle):

Indoor:
Religious Facility
Hall
Special Venue
Barn

Outdoor:
Garden
Backyard
Special Venue
Park

You May Now Kiss the Bride! Put Lipstick on and Kiss the Page All Over!

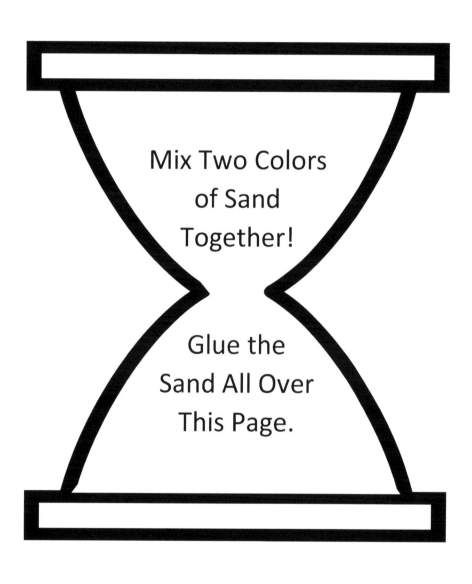

The DJ Requested a List of Your Favorite Songs.

Use These Clues to Seat Each Person at the Right Table on the Next Page!

a. Evelyn is friends with the bride, she is a sweetheart and can sit anywhere, but prefers to sit at table 1.
b. Jade needs to sit next to Grandma GiGi to catch up on things.
c. Charlie must sit at table 3. No questions asked.
d. Felix is a friend of the groom and is trying to ask Cousin Taylor on a date.
e. Jason is sitting at table 2 and is married to Jade.
f. Uncle Sebastian isn't allowed at the wedding.
g. Cousin Jack is best friends with Charlie.
h. Evelyn is sitting next to Aunt Suzy.
i. Jade can't stand Uncle Dylan's chewing.
j. Cousin Hayden and Cousin Grace are Cousin Jack's Siblings.
k. Ivy is sitting at table 2.
l. Aunt Suzy is Married to Uncle Rodrick.
m. Aunt Nova is crazy, so is her 3 kids.
n. Cousin Taylor is looking forward to catching up with Evelyn who she hasn't seen in a while.
o. Lucas came with Ivy.
p. Cousin Lucy is Cousin Taylors Sister.
q. Obviously, Grandma and Grandpa need to be by each other.

Cut and Glue These on the Next Page, Make Sure They are at The Correct Table!

- Cousin Grace
- Jade
- Felix
- Grandma GiGi
- Cousin Lucy
- Uncle Rodrick
- Evelyn
- Lucas
- Jason
- Aunt Nova
- Uncle Sebastian
- Cousin Taylor
- Cousin Hayden
- Uncle Dylan
- Ivy
- Charlie
- Cousin Jack
- Grandpa Fred
- Aunt Suzy

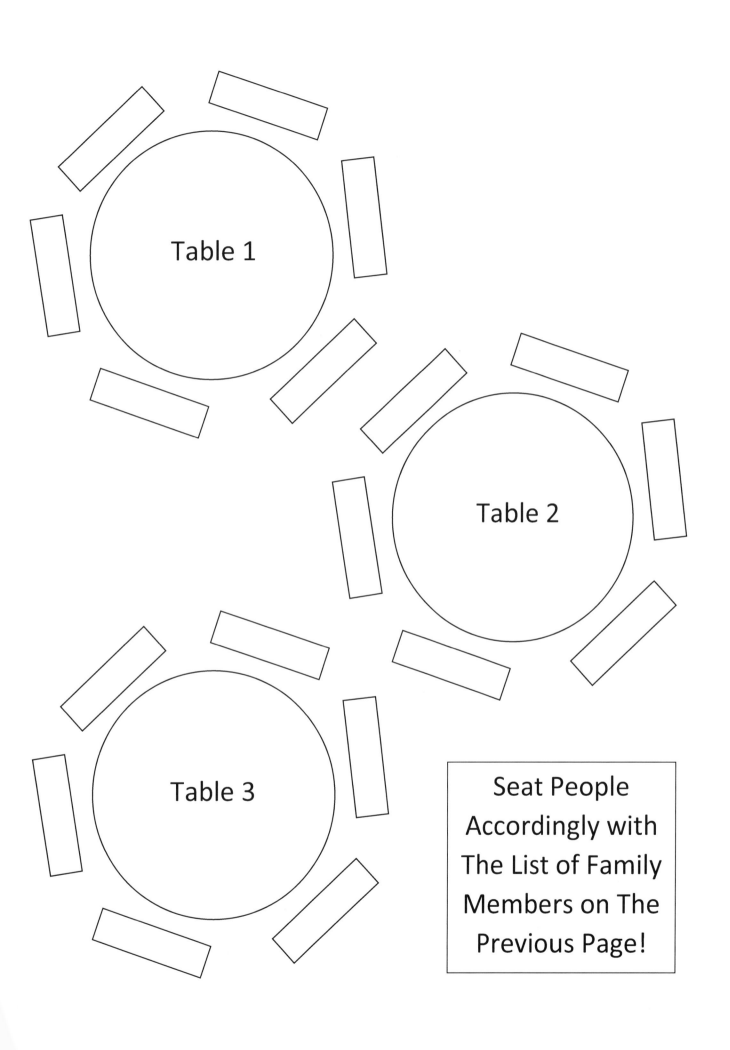

Decorate Your Wedding Planner Cover!

Create a Scrapbook Telling Your Love Story

Who is Sitting at Your Rehearsal Dinner Table?

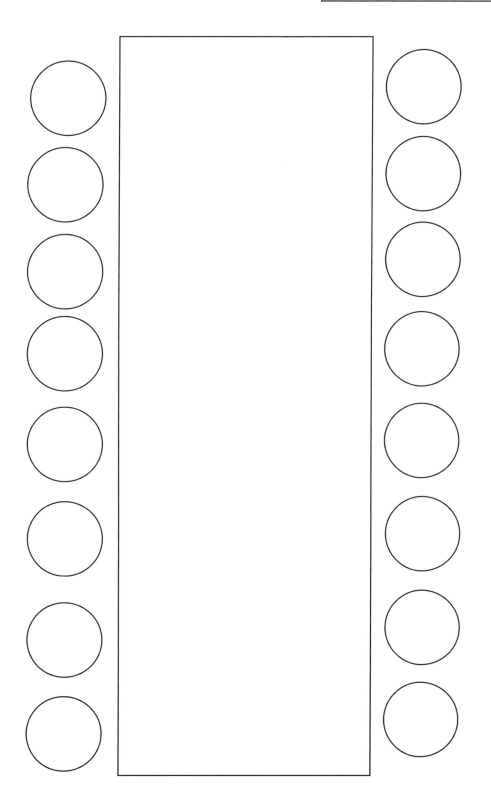

Tie the Knot! Color these Knots According to Your Color Swatch!

What Does Your Dream Invitation Look Like?

What are You Wearing?

DRESS:

Wedding Gown Color:

_____

Wedding Gown Silhouette:

A-Line	Sheath	Trumpet
Ballgown	Mermaid	

Neckline:

Straight Across	High Neck	Illusion
Asymmetric	Spaghetti Strap	Off-Shoulder Illusion
Sweetheart	Off-Shoulder	Square
Semi-Sweetheart	Queen Anne	Halter Strap

Sleeve Style:

Strapless Spaghetti	Short	Long Sleeve
Cap	3/4 Sleeve	

Back of Dress:

U-Shape	Closed	V-Shape
Bare	Open	X-Cross

Veil Style:

_____

Bridal Shoes:

_____

Bridal Accessories:

_____

Hairstyle:

_____

What Does Your Wedding Day Pedicure Look Like?

Set a Timer for Two Minutes and See How Many Wedding Related Words You Can Write Down!

Let's Plan the Parties!

Bachelorette:

Where?

Theme?

Who is Invited?

What are we doing?

Budget?

Bachelor:

Where?

Theme?

Who is Invited?

What are we doing?

Budget?

Practice Signing Your New Name!

High Heels are Overrated! Bedazzle the Shoe!

Write Your Wedding Vows to Your Future Spouse on This Page!

Write Your Ideas for Each Thing in the Box!

Something Old

Something New

Something Borrowed

Something Blue

I DO Want to Decorate This Page.

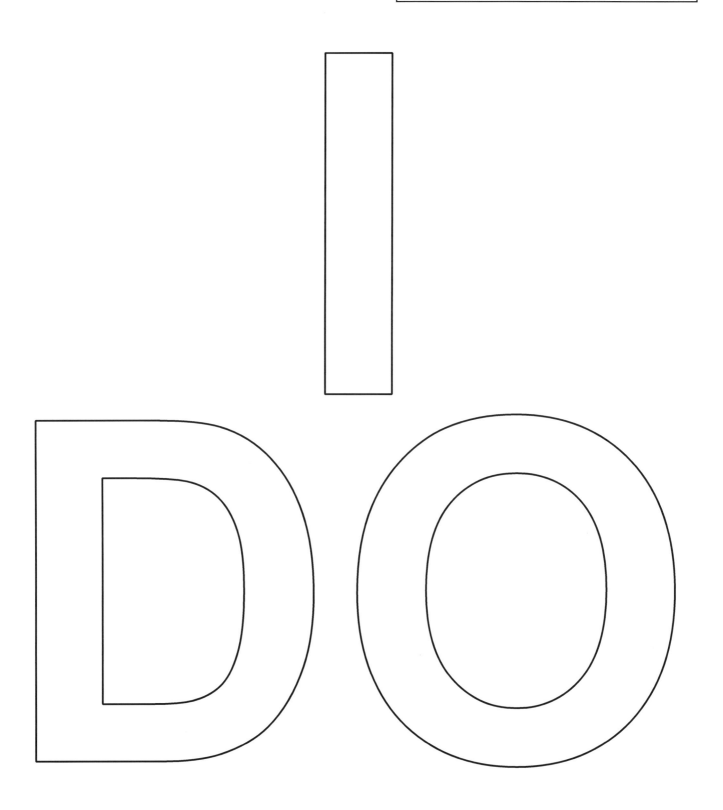

Describe Your Dream Spouse on This Page!

What Do Your Wedding Nails Look Like? Don't Forget the Ring!

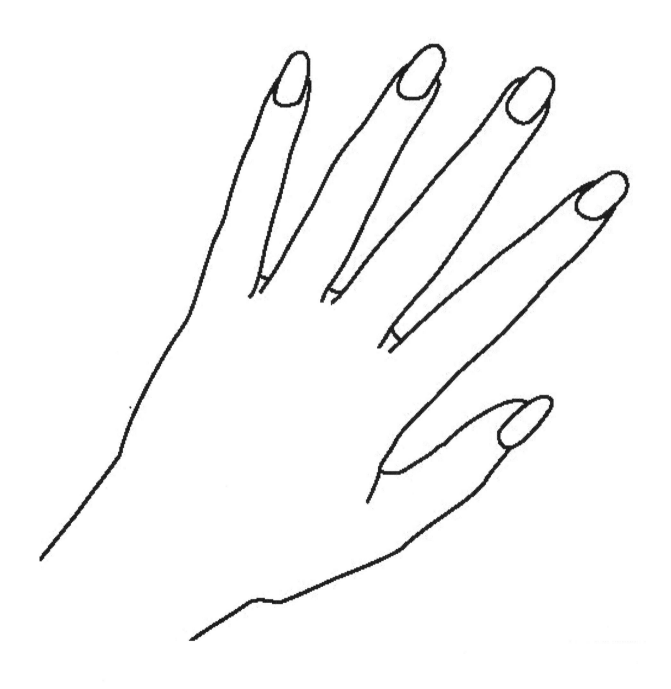

Decorate Your Infinity Symbol.

Rice Send Off! Cover This Page with Glue. Throw Rice at the Page Until it is Covered!

Made in the USA
Columbia, SC
29 December 2021